THE WORLD BENEATH THE SEA

THE WORLD BENEATH THE SEA

SUSAN HARRIS

An Easy-Read Fact Book

Franklin Watts
New York I London I 1979

Illustrated by Tony Gibbons and Alan Male

Thanks are due to the following for kind permission to reproduce photographs:

Heather Angel; Australian High Commission; Canadian High Commission; Central Office of Information; El Al; Bill Holden; Keystone Press Agency; Mansell Collection; Marineland, Florida; Ministry of Agriculture, Fisheries and Food; Ministry of Defence; NASA; Neco Communications Limited; Radio Times Hulton Picture Library; Sea Mammal Research Unit; Seaphot Limited; United States Travel Service; Vickers

Library of Congress Cataloging in Publication Data

Harris, Susan.
    The world beneath the sea.

    (An Easy-read fact book)
    Includes index.
    SUMMARY: Briefly examines the ocean's currents, floor, vegetation, and animal life. Includes a discussion of underwater exploration.
    1. Marine biology—Juvenile literature. 2. Ocean—Juvenile literature. [1. Marine biology. 2. Ocean. 3. Underwater exploration] I. Gibbons, Tony. II. Male, Alan. III. Title.
QH91.16.H37   551.4′6   78-10880
ISBN 0-531-02854-2

R.L. 2.8 Spache Revised Formula

View of the earth from space.

The earth is a very watery place.

In fact, over three quarters of our world is covered with water.

Some of this water is in rivers and lakes. But most of it is found in **oceans** (O-shuns).

Ocean, or sea, water is different from lake water. Sea water is very **salty**.

This saltiness has come about in two ways.

As rivers flow over land, they pick up many **minerals**. One of these minerals is salt.

As the water dries up (evaporates), salt is left behind.

Salt also comes from the ocean floor.

The salt in the rocks melts in the sea water.

Water cycle

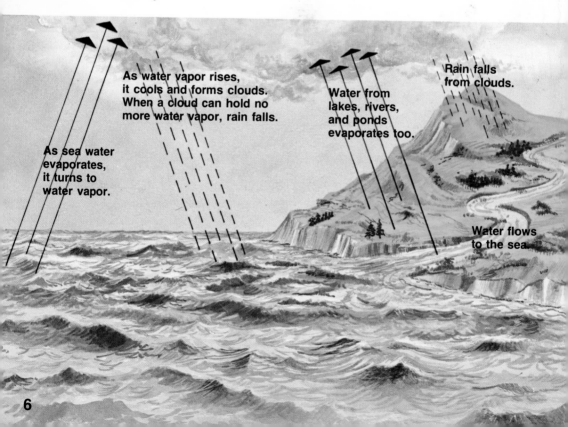

As water vapor rises, it cools and forms clouds. When a cloud can hold no more water vapor, rain falls.

As sea water evaporates, it turns to water vapor.

Water from lakes, rivers, and ponds evaporates too.

Rain falls from clouds.

Water flows to the sea.

The Dead Sea

Some seas are saltier than others.

There is a sea in Israel called the **Dead Sea**. Its water is so salty that few things can live in it.

The Baltic Sea is in northern Europe. Its water is much less salty.

This is because its entrance is so small. The salty seas around it cannot flow into it very easily.

The waters of the seas are always moving. Some of these movements are called **currents**.

Currents are formed when warm and cold water meet. Cold water is heavier than warm water. So it sinks and flows under the warmer water.

Currents carry heat and cold from one place to another.

For this reason, they have a great effect on the weather.

Ocean currents. The pale blue arrows show warm currents. The dark blue arrows show cold currents.

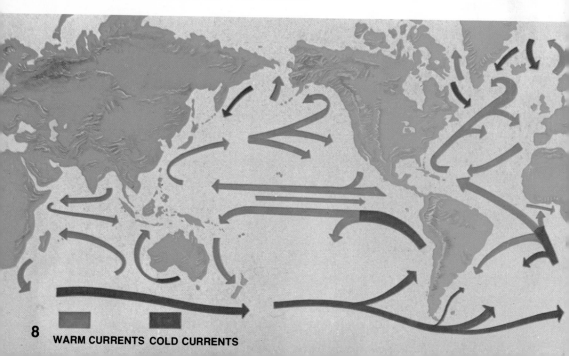

WARM CURRENTS COLD CURRENTS

Icebreaker in Canada

The warm **Gulf Stream** flows past western Europe. This is why some countries there have mild climates.

The Gulf Stream reaches Norway. So most of the harbors there stay ice-free during the winter.

But Labrador, in Canada, has frozen harbors all winter. Labrador is further south than Norway, but it is not warmed by the Gulf Stream.

The movement of water is also caused by **tides**.

Tides are caused by the pull of the moon and the sun.

The water directly under the moon is pulled by the moon's **gravity**. This pull causes a rise in water called **high tide**.

The water furthest from the moon is pulled the least. **Low tides** occur here.

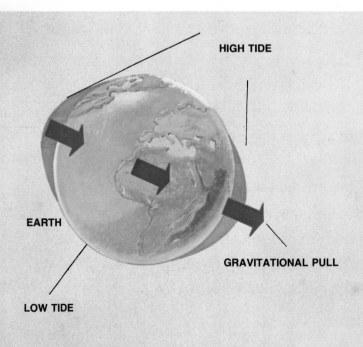

HIGH TIDE

EARTH

GRAVITATIONAL PULL

LOW TIDE

MOON

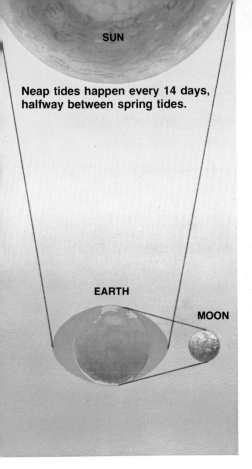

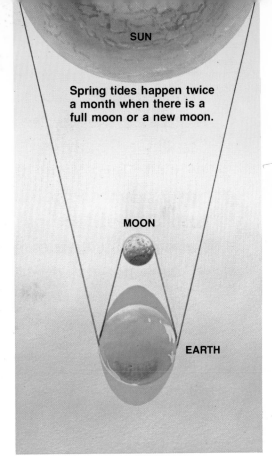

Neap tides happen every 14 days, halfway between spring tides.

SUN

EARTH

MOON

Spring tides happen twice a month when there is a full moon or a new moon.

SUN

MOON

EARTH

Sometimes the sun, moon, and earth form an "L" shape.

At these times, the pull is weak. The tides are lowest. They are called **neap** (NEEP) **tides**.

But sometimes the sun, earth, and moon are in a straight line. Then the pull is stronger, and the tides are bigger. These are called **spring tides**.

Tides vary from place to place.

The tides of the Mediterranean Sea are very small.

The Bay of Fundy, in Canada, has the highest tides of all. Twice a day, the waters rise 40 feet (12 m) inside the Bay.

Sailors need to know all about tides.

Large ships usually enter or leave a port at high tide. The water is deepest then.

The Royal Yacht *Britannia* **entering Sydney Harbor at high tide**

A surfer rides a wave off the coast of Hawaii.

Wind also moves sea water. This causes **waves**. Some waves may travel thousands of miles before crashing onto a beach. These waves are good for surfing.

The deepest parts of the ocean are called **trenches**. They are long, narrow valleys with clifflike walls.

The Marianas Trench is in the western Pacific Ocean. It is one of the deepest trenches. It is 36,000 feet (10,975 m) deep.

Early sailors used a lead line to measure the depth of water.

Today scientists use an **echo sounder**. This measures the times it takes a sound to bounce back from the ocean floor.

A sailor about to throw a lead line

A trace taken from an echo sounder

9,000 FT. (2743 M)

The Mindanao Deep is near the Philippine Islands. There the ocean floor is 37,772 feet (11,516 m) deep.

18,000 FT. (5486 M)

27,000 FT. (8229 M)

37,772 FT. (11,516 M)

The ocean floor is not just flat.

There are muddy plains and deep valleys.

There are even rocky mountain ranges.

The part of the ocean floor next to the continents is called the **continental shelf**.

The part that falls away sharply is called the **continental slope**.

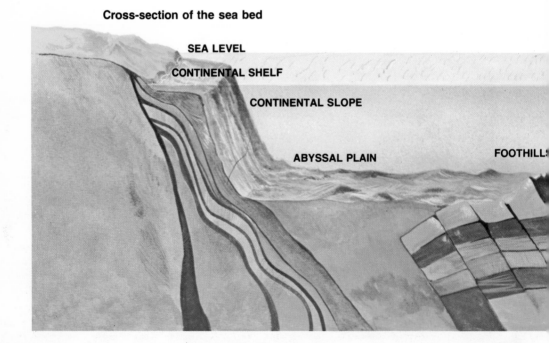

Cross-section of the sea bed

SEA LEVEL

CONTINENTAL SHELF

CONTINENTAL SLOPE

ABYSSAL PLAIN

FOOTHILL

For miles beyond the continental slope, the ocean floor is flat. This is called the **abyssal plain** (a-BIS-al PLANE).

Then the land slowly rises into undersea hills. Beyond the hills are tall undersea mountains. They make up a **mid-ocean ridge**.

In the middle is a long valley called a **mid-ocean rift**.

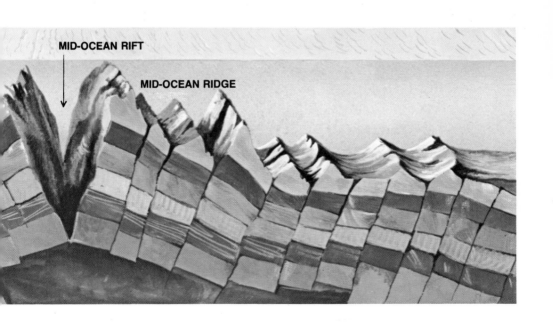

MID-OCEAN RIFT

MID-OCEAN RIDGE

Sometimes the mountaintops of ocean ridges rise above the surface of the water.

Some islands are formed in this way.

Coral reefs sometimes form around these islands.

Coral is made from the skeletons of tiny animals called **coral polyps** (KOR-al POL-ips).

Life in a coral reef

Coral reefs around an island break the force of the waves.

They make a sheltered area for plants and fish.

These diagrams show how a coral island is formed.

1. The coral grows around the edge of an island.
The skeletons build up on top of each other.

2. At the same time, the island is wearing away.

3. A new island is formed from coral around the edge of the old island.
In the center is a lagoon (a pool of quiet water).

The sea is home to many plants and animals. Some of the smallest are called **plankton** (PLANK-ton).

Plankton (magnified about 700 times)

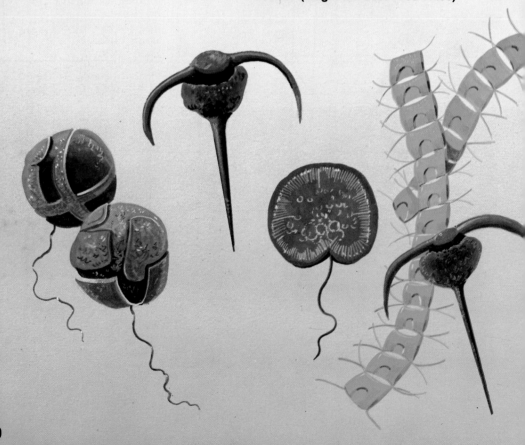

20

Plankton is made up of tiny plants and animals that drift near the water surface.

It forms the basic food for the other animals of the sea.

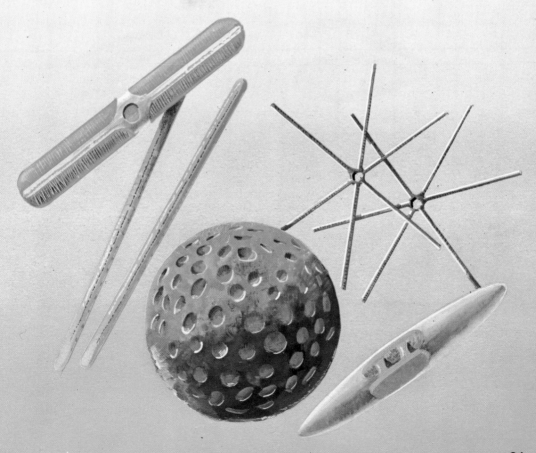

Life on the seashore is hard. Creatures living there must protect themselves from the pounding waves.

Some creatures, such as limpets and mussels, live in shells.

Others, such as shrimps and crabs, bury themselves in sand.

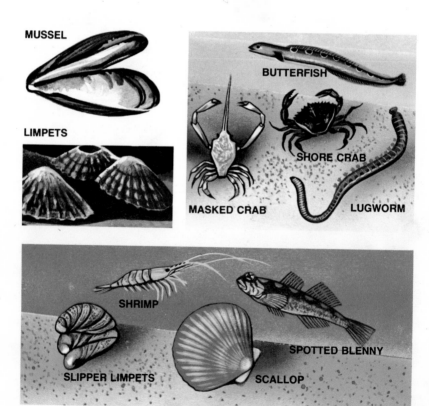

MUSSEL

LIMPETS

BUTTERFISH

SHORE CRAB

MASKED CRAB

LUGWORM

SHRIMP

SLIPPER LIMPETS

SCALLOP

SPOTTED BLENNY

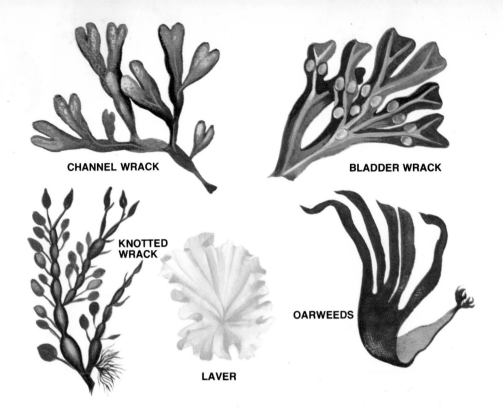

CHANNEL WRACK

BLADDER WRACK

KNOTTED WRACK

OARWEEDS

LAVER

Seaweeds are simple plants. They have no leaves or flowers.

They protect themselves with a thick, rubbery skin.

Most seaweeds attach themselves to rocks on the ocean floor.

There are many types of plants and animals in the ocean. They are all important.

Plankton is a source of food for small fish. These fish are then eaten by larger fish.

When the larger fish die, they decay on the ocean floor.

Their minerals help plankton to grow.

This pattern is called a **food chain**.

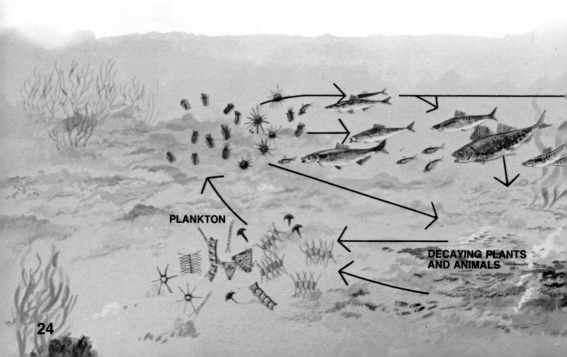

PLANKTON

DECAYING PLANTS
AND ANIMALS

It is very important that nothing destroys any part of the food chain.

One way of destroying the food chain is by over-fishing.

Also, some countries dump wastes into the sea. This makes the water **polluted** (pol-LU-ted), or dirty.

Enough pollution can kill fish and plants.

Sometimes fish become poisoned by pollution. Then they pass the poison on to the people who eat them.

Food chain

Far below the water surface, at a depth of 490 to 1,640 feet (150 to 492 m), is a part of the ocean called the **midwater** area.

There is very little light here.

Some of the fish in this area have special light organs to help them see.

These organs are called **photophores**
(PHO-to-fores).

Other midwater fish have very big eyes. These
help them see in the little light there is.

The deepest part of the ocean is known as the **abyss** (a-BIS). No sunlight reaches this area. There are no plants, and it is very cold.

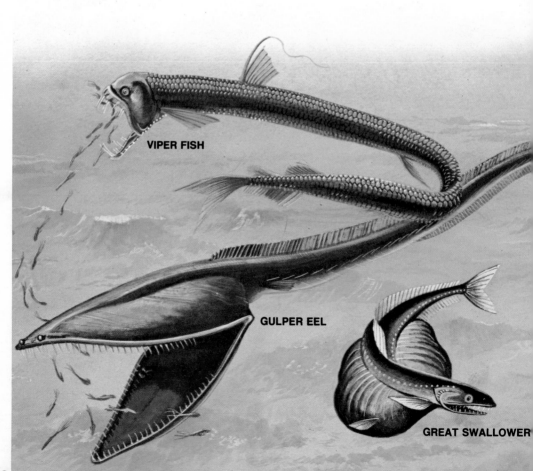

VIPER FISH

GULPER EEL

GREAT SWALLOWER

The animals here live in darkness. So they have very small eyes. But they have a very good sense of smell.

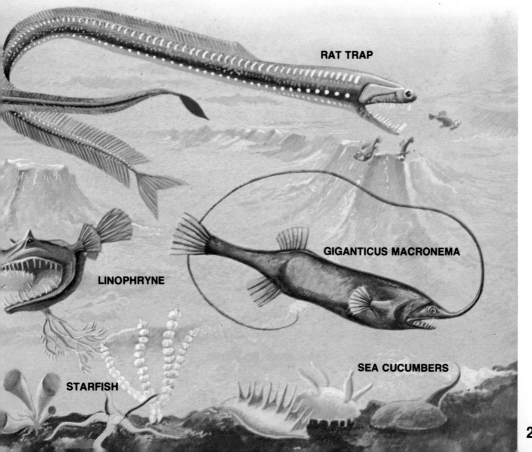

RAT TRAP

GIGANTICUS MACRONEMA

LINOPHRYNE

SEA CUCUMBERS

STARFISH

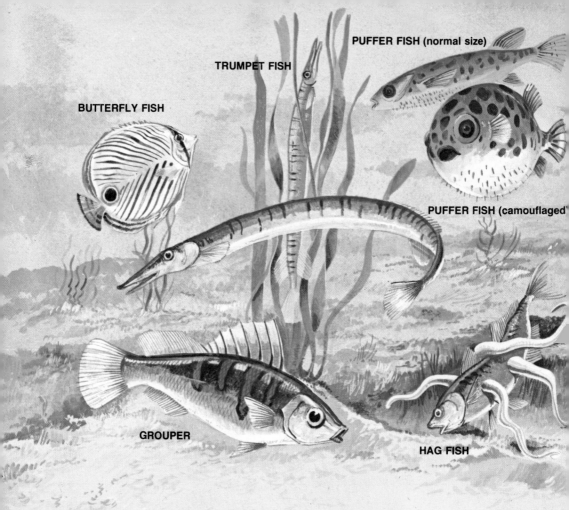

BUTTERFLY FISH

TRUMPET FISH

PUFFER FISH (normal size)

PUFFER FISH (camouflaged)

GROUPER

HAG FISH

One of the ways fish protect themselves is through **camouflage** (KAM-o-flahj).

This means they can look or act like something else.

Trumpet fish look like one of the weeds they hide in.

Puffer fish can blow themselves up into a ball.

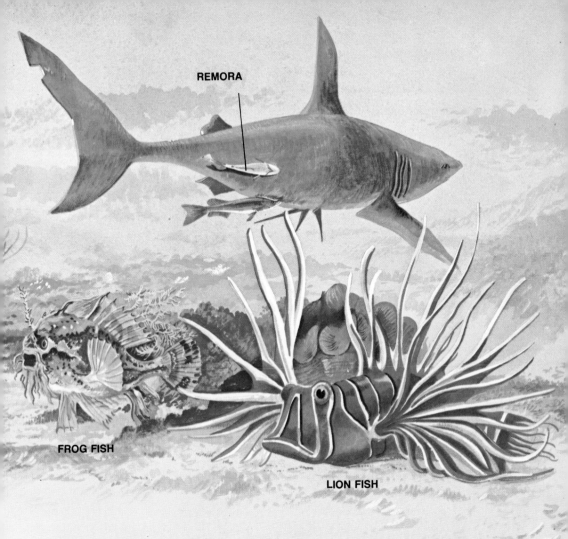

REMORA

FROG FISH

LION FISH

The frog fish looks like a big piece of seaweed.
And some groupers can change colors instantly.
They can also change from spots to stripes at the
same time.

The octopus and the squid are two unusual creatures.

The octopus has eight **tentacles** (TENT-e-kles). It wraps these around its food.

Most squid are small creatures. But they are powerful swimmers.

Octopus. *(Inset)* **Close-up of tentacle**

ENEMY   **SQUID**

First the squid changes to a dark color.

It shoots out a cloud of dark fluid.
The squid then changes back to a light color.

The enemy becomes confused.
It follows the dark cloud,
while the squid escapes.

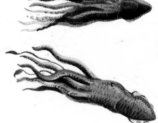

Squid have a very special way of protecting themselves.

First, they turn from a light to a dark color.

Then they shoot out a cloud of dark liquid. This fools the enemy.

While the enemy attacks the dark fluid, the squid swims safely away.

Fish often move from one area to another. This is called **migration** (mi-GRAY-shun).

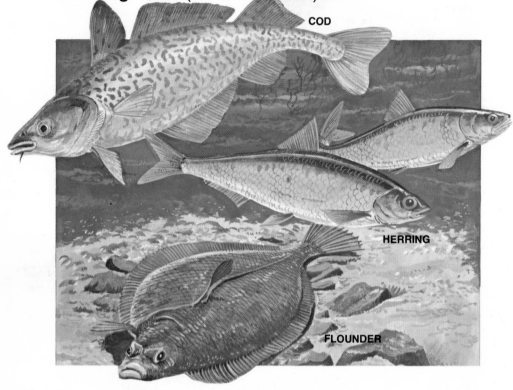

COD

HERRING

FLOUNDER

Scientists find this out by first catching a fish. They tag it with a plastic label. Then they return it to the sea.

When it is caught again, scientists can tell how far it swam.

The Atlantic salmon (SAM-mon) can migrate nearly 2,000 miles (3,200 km).

It starts out in the Atlantic Ocean. Then it swims to rivers all over Europe and eastern North America to lay its eggs.

Tagging has shown that salmon return to the same river every year.

Tagging fish

SALMON

Another large and interesting fish is the shark.

Sharks have huge, powerful jaws. Many have sharp teeth.

There may be five or six rows of teeth in all. Sometimes a front tooth drops out. Then a back tooth simply moves into its place!

Close-up of a shark's head

Tiger shark

Sharks have to swim in order to breathe. So they never stop moving.

Most sharks eat only plankton and other small creatures.

They strain their food through their teeth.

But some larger sharks will attack people. The white shark and the tiger shark have been known to eat swimmers.

The largest sea creatures of all are whales. Although they look like big fish, they are not fish.

Whales are mammals. Like people, they are warm blooded. And they feed their young with their own milk.

Whales actually communicate. But not with words. They use high-pitched whistles and squeaks.

Some dolphins have been trained to do tricks.

Whaling station, with finback whale on the left, and sei (SAY) whale on the right.
(Inset) **Close-up of mouth of finback whale, showing baleen.**

There are many different kinds of whales. Dolphins are a kind of whale. They have teeth. But many large whales don't have teeth.

Some have baleen (ba-LEEN).

This is a kind of fringe that grows from their upper jaws.

Because people have killed so many whales, some types are in danger of **extinction** (ex-TINK-shun). This means there are not many left.

But the ocean holds something other than animal and plant life.

There are also many minerals under the sea. One of the most important minerals is **oil**.

Oil is removed from the ocean floor with huge drilling rigs. Then it is sent to refineries, where it is made into fuel.

◀ **Oil rig off the coast of Australia**

Natural gas is often found when drilling for oil. It is used in homes and factories.

Diver examining shipwreck at the bottom of the Indian Ocean

Sometimes the oceans hold other kinds of riches.

Divers looking for shipwrecks have sometimes found money and jewels.

But even more important, shipwrecks can teach us about history.

Sunken ships can tell us a lot about people who lived long ago.

Ancient stone carving showing underwater swimmers

People swam underwater nearly 3,000 years ago. They carried air bags made of animal skins.

But exploring the seas would not be possible without modern equipment.

Today divers wear flippers to help them move fast. They wear goggles in order to see clearly. And they wear wet suits to stay warm.

They breathe through air tanks strapped to their backs.

During the 1930s, the **bathysphere** (BATH-e-sphere) was invented. It was a large steel ball with glass windows.

It was lowered into the sea on a steel cable. The cable was attached to a boat.

Divers in a bathysphere could stay underwater for a few hours.

A bathysphere

**Bathyscaphe being lowered into the sea
from its support ship**

Today much more complex machines are used.
The **bathyscaphe** (BATH-e-skaf) allows scientists
to stay underwater for several days.
There they can study the ocean floor and
underwater animal life.

Underwater houses, such as Sealabs (SEE-LABS), have been developed.

They are made to find out how long people can live and work under the sea.

So far, people have lived in Sealabs for many weeks.

The HMS *Dreadnought*, **a nuclear submarine.**
(Inset) **Controls inside submarine**

The largest underwater craft of all are **submarines** (sub-ma-REENS).

Modern submarines can carry a hundred people or more.

Until recently, most submarines ran on diesel fuel and electricity.

Today, however, modern submarines use **nuclear energy** (NU-cle-ar EN-er-gy). This allows them to stay underwater for long periods of time.

Early sea explorers returned home saying that they had seen huge monsters. The sea was mysterious and frightening to them.

With modern equipment, we are learning more and more about the sea.

We still don't know everything about it. We know that large and unusual fish do exist. But we can be fairly sure that there are no "monsters."

Index